A Day with George

The Sound of Soft G

By Cynthia Amoroso

2

I babysit a boy named George.

George shows me his giraffe.

George shows
me his gerbil.

George has
a gentle puppy.

9

10

George wants
gingerbread
cookies.

We wash germs off our hands.

13

After eating, we go to the gym.

We see a giant ball at the gym.

17

George sees his friend Gene.

George picks
a geranium to
thank me for
a fun day.

Word List:

Gene	giant
gentle	gingerbread
George	giraffe
geranium	gym
gerbil	
germs	

Note to Parents and Educators

The books in this series are based on current research, which supports the idea that our brains are pattern-detectors rather than rules-appliers. This means children learn to read easier when they are taught the familiar spelling patterns found in English. As children encounter more complex words, they have greater success in figuring out these words by using the spelling patterns.

Throughout the series, the texts provide the reader with the opportunity to practice and apply knowledge of the sounds in natural language. The books introduce sounds using familiar onsets and *rimes*, or spelling patterns, for reinforcement.

For example, the word *cat* might be used to present the short "a" sound, with the letter *c* being the onset and "_at" being the rime. This approach provides practice and reinforcement of the short "a" sound, as there are many familiar words made with the "_at" rime.

The stories and accompanying photographs in this series are based on time-honored concepts in children's literature: well-written, engaging texts and colorful, high-quality photographs combine to produce books that children want to read again and again.

Dr. Peg Ballard
Minnesota State University, Mankato

Published by The Child's World®
1980 Lookout Drive • Mankato, MN 56003-1705
800-599-READ • www.childsworld.com

ACKNOWLEDGMENTS
The Child's World®: Mary Swensen, Publishing Director
The Design Lab: Design
Michael Miller: Editing

PHOTO CREDITS
© 3445128471/Shutterstock.com: 13; Bjørn Hovdal/
Dreamstime.com: 10; Denis Kovin/Shutterstock.com: 5;
Dmitrij Skorobogatov/Shutterstock.com: 17; Jagodka/
Shutterstock.com: 9; KPG_Payless/Shutterstock.com: 21;
Kuttelvaserova Stuchelova/Shutterstock.com: 6; Lopolo/
Shutterstock.com: cover, 2; Syda Productions/Shutterstock.
com: 18; Vereshchagin Dmitry/Shutterstock.com: 14

ISBN 9781503809314
LCCN 2015958473

Printed in the United States of America
PA02430

ABOUT THE AUTHOR

Cynthia Amoroso holds undergraduate
degrees in English and elementary educa-
tion, and graduate degrees in curriculum
and instruction as well as educational ad-
ministration. She is currently an assistant
superintendent in a suburban metropolitan
school district. Cynthia's past roles include
teacher, assistant principal, district reading
coordinator, director of curriculum and
instruction, and curriculum consultant.
She has extensive experience in reading,
literacy, curriculum development, pro-
fessional development, and continuous
improvement processes.